Anatomy Museum

Erin Cisney

Anatomy Museum

Erin Cisney

ANATOMY MUSEUM
Copyright©2020 Erin Cisney
All Rights Reserved
Published by Unsolicited Press
Printed in the United States of America.
First Edition 2020.

All rights reserved. Printed in the United States of America. No part of this book may be used or reproduced in any manner whatsoever without written permission except in the case of brief quotations embodied in critical articles or reviews.

Attention schools and businesses: for discounted copies on large orders, please contact the publisher directly. Books are brought to the trade by Ingram.

For information contact:
Unsolicited Press
Portland, Oregon
www.unsolicitedpress.com
orders@unsolicitedpress.com
619-354-8005

Cover Design: Kathryn Gerhardt
Editor: Rebekah Stogner; S.R. Stewart
ISBN: 978-1-950730-34-6

Acknowledgements

"Electrical Storm," "I'm So Tired," and "Sour" were originally published by *Camroc Press Review*.

"Crystal Park" was originally published by *Rust + Moth*.

"Anatomy" was originally published by *Literary Orphans*.

"Votive" and "Jamaica Honeymoon" were originally published by *VAYAVA*.

Poems

Poems	7
Electrical Storm	8
Crystal Park	9
High School	10
Blues	11
Sunday	13
Eidetic	14
Camp	15
The Neptune	16
A One-Sided Conversation	17
15	18
Sour	19
Anatomy	20
I'm So Tired	22
Patient	23
Crush	24
July	25
This Is the End	26
Votive	27
Jamaica Honeymoon	28
Haunting the House	30

Electrical Storm

Night clots in blue-black and hums nostalgic,
telephone wires caught by wind snake on walls,
frantic, barely tethered. I'm obsessed with regrets.

Clouds collide and spark, trees ripple.
Our sheets thrash under a fan that spins so fast
it rocks back and forth in its plaster socket,
threatens to buck loose from the ceiling.

Is it raining where you are? I shake him awake.
My damp hair is cold, smooth like riverbed stone,
sprays in tentacles across his stomach.

In the faceless dark, I'm a chasm, bottomless,
the sky groans on in ominous minor key.
I want, want unspeakable things, floods, catastrophe.

Crystal Park

The park where I swing at midnight,
where I sometimes choke on pills,
and boys hide glitter-eyed in the pavilion
calling me by my red hair, asking for a light.
A lifetime laced across the picnic table,
fortunes scratched in splintered wood
while clammy-handed, impatient, I catch fire,
my mouth around a metal pipe.
In times like these, it helps to be
moon-vacant and crystal-cut,
anyone's convenient circumstance
hidden in public space.
Chain-link glides icy smooth, painful
between fingertips. Touch me
and I'll keep secrets.
Like the playground I can be
tagged with any name, vandalized
and given new meaning.

High School

The strip mall has been vacated, lies empty.

Two teenagers make out
in the back row, the movie
is beautiful and subtitled.

In the back of the class, a boy
sells prescriptions for your heavy heart.

Empty is another word for sick.
My father is hollow, doesn't believe
in coincidences or second chances.

I've had a few close calls,
don't always do what's right.

Blues

Shaving my legs in the baby blue bathtub,
drunk on Bacardi and shaving my legs
behind the plastic sky blue curtain
(bad idea to shave your legs drunk)

and the razor catches at the bump of my knee
and red runs down my white shin,
red on white and red on blue, a ribbon
of red on white and blue.

Kenny's a nice boy, he means well.
And he meant well when he sat me down
on the edge of the powder blue sink
and fumbled into me on tiptoe,

neon blue toothpaste smearing
the back of my sundress.
He meant well but was excited
and he would've kissed me

if he weren't so excited,
but he was so excited
he reached out with his right hand
and wrapped it around my throat,

pushed and slammed the back of my head
into the medicine cabinet and the mirror
shattered into a million shards
of a million different hues of blue.

Sunday

Addiction does not fill an absence,
it creates an absence

where something terrible used to be.
Christ, tell me something I don't know.

On Sundays I wouldn't answer the phone.

I will redact
I will start over
I am not the sum of my parents

My addiction is ridiculous
and overrated. I am a terrible
sum of consequence. The bed
is a carnivore with iron teeth.

Christ, it's so terrible.
Addiction, staring down
into your sock drawer, lonely,
can't catch a break.

The phone would ring and ring,
I wouldn't answer.

Eidetic

Dark   stacked on top of us
in beaten blues,   summer
thick against a single pane
as our legs   hitch together
in soft shapes of subtle construction.
We are so young and full of fear,
red exclamations of excess heat.
By degrees   .we'll learn everything,
How to swim with grace,
      how many stars will fill a sky.

Camp

You were rough and sometimes
I was ashamed to be seen with you.
Sometimes I'd imagine parents made of paper
with sun halos, confident swimmers.

Our camp is falling apart and you're
lighting a sparkler held in your teeth,
a free spirit, unconcerned with weather
or bad news because I fear enough for us both.

The moon was thick and circumspect,
brutally bright, showering the pines
in uneasy forecasts, a long,
hard road in the dark.

The Neptune

Seasick, I spill from a passenger seat
in dark glasses, penitent and green gilled,
blinded by the glint of jade and amber glass confetti
strewn over this parking lot of a lousy diner.
A crumb of glass skips into my flip-flop
and burrows deep into my heel
while I maintain good humor through clenched teeth.
In the restroom, I fish it out of my foot
with tweezers, think, "These weekends
will be the death of me," and remember
that this is only temporary, beating the blues out
until I'm grateful again, this big disappointment.
I return to the booth, show the gravel sized glass bit,
still bloody, to my crew in an open palm and say,
"See this? It was in me, I got it out."

A One-Sided Conversation

He was the boy who didn't speak,
he was perfectly silent. Perfect,
as a black shadow in his blacker bedroom.

I tried to pull words out of him
like a vacuum. My tongue
searched in the dark
for a sweet spot or loose nerve

while worlds away, my name
reverberated in empty shells,
a phone rang with no answer.

But I was preoccupied and determined,
haunted by palm lines,
a dial tone away from forever.

15

I reach for a little fresh perspective
above the refrigerator.

I'm a lonely girl, I've got problems.
And this house is so empty, makes me nervous
like the absence of a pulse. Underneath the quiet,
I can almost hear God packing his bags, saying
my work here will soon be done.

Drinking is the next best thing
to fucking or getting stoned.
When I drink I feel beautiful
like anemones waving under water,
like floating pink fronds, nebulous.

Here's a cure for being cored, for leaving
yourself naked on the dance floor,
sending out too many invitations, high
expectations and the cold, hard slap
they were received with. Bottles,
bottles of pure, white light,
a toast to the ghosts we cling to.

Sour

I

I was, quite honestly, a disappointment,
prone to poor decisions, spectacular naivete,
a slave to the teenage complex,
and I remember the moment you lost faith in me,
midnight, December of the new millennium,
another year looming with malicious intent.

II

The last words you say to your father
will never be satisfactory in retrospect.
Keep it simple.

III

What was it you were whispering?
Middle of the night, somber,
plotting my future? Dropout?
Teenage mother? Do I miss you?
Guilt-ridden or vindictive,
whatever my reasons,
ten years and I still haven't visited.

Anatomy

Slow songs and addiction
were filling a hole in me.
Empty, what I desperately

wanted to be. My father's throat
laced with white, cannibal vines
that glowed in the dark.

Only he could see them.
Plants were dying on the sill.
I opened up my calves

like a sunrise full of red.
When he died, I bought fish,
I filled an aquarium with cichlids

and suckermouths,
watched them swim.
Spring was too bright,

the tulips and hyacinths,
unsympathetic, blooming
with vicious force.

In dreams I was lost
in anatomy museums
surrounded by secrets

on display, obscene and quiet.
Imagine the colors beneath your skin,
how fragile the filigree of nerves.

When he died, I stopped believing
in ghosts. I grew up, studied biology,
drank clear liquor to feel clean.

I'm So Tired

hello brick wall, cratered planet, dusty corners,
28 has been so dull, dead weight,
another box of junk in the attic.

jesus, no one tries anymore,
not like we used to, spit and sparked
with so much trying, lit each other up.
goodbye impulse, goodbye feathered past.

now spiders wait until the lights go out,
wander up from the basement,
tiptoe politely along the baseboards,
moths beat screens, but softly, barely a whisper
of summer thrashings. we drink heavy,
talk of rain, rust in our sleep.

Patient

The moon was like a razor,
calm and full of spite,
but simply put I feared you,
your confidence and carefully laid plans.

In December, the birds left
in a hurricane of feathers,
the sky, mute and empty.

The slow tilt of atmosphere
is less noticeable in the north
where stars never change.

Let numbers fall from their pages,
let the sky keep spinning while we sleep.

We'll meet again in an empty field
after the crows have flown home,
after you've come to your senses.

Crush

Here you are, criminal heartthrob,
bringing a shot glass to your lips
as if years only solidified your place
over the mantel of so many
candles lit in schoolgirl bedrooms.
Blood hurricanes, reluctant tremors.
There's an effortless calm involved
in being so tragic, so capable
of falling off the edge of the earth
at any moment. With an inordinate sense
of accomplishment, I lit your cigarettes
under the blue neon of false hopes,
walked along the cracks of your fault lines
with heavy tread and determination.

July

Late, yellow lamp light
in midnight ink, branches
holding up a white moon
like fruit. It's July
and we're careless.

Summer is wet
on my skin, breathing
suburban timelessness
on a back porch, someone's
childhood home.

Am I so forgettable? Nights
spent in hopeful company,
searching through sky
with a dead syllable
on my tongue, a memory

questionable and charming,
just past the point of recall.
In the dark, a man fumbles
for a light, says my name
like an expectation.

This Is the End

The morning after the world was supposed to end
I woke naked, hungover, alone on your side of the bed
and the wind was apocalyptic in its own right,
the sound as it tore through the city a warning
that the end will come soon but not as predicted.

I'm accustomed to the coolly judgmental stare of ghosts
like an acid bath or the doomsday red of emergency lights,
but I think, "Where's the mercy in all this, the moral?"
Predictable, rushing towards the last page as usual.

When I'm alone the thought that I could do anything
paralyzes me with its possibilities and I may sit here
in indecision for a very long time with the sound
of this new wind tearing siding off our house,
the break of dawn, just another day's miracle.

Votive

That pinprick of empty
a wormhole where your heart was.

I never wanted to be so sentimental
but this moonlit single pillow,

the empty cathedral at midnight.
Goddamn, it's like . . .

It's like memory is a multitude of tiny toads
escaping from underfoot,

like the clink of tiny claws
in the walls at night.

The past blooms
on the other side of a keyhole,

and I've been turning boys' pockets
inside out

searching for keys.

Jamaica Honeymoon

It's been some struggle
walking barefoot across
so much beach in the dark,

the suck of sand,
a black surf's deposit
of broken shell bits

along its foam edge.
Still, this drunken
good humor, everything

new and made for us,
no matter how imperfectly,
ours. I stop to pick

a cigarette butt from
between my toes
and a cat rushes up

unafraid and eager
to lick dinner's grease
from our palms.

It bleeds from a slash
across one eye, this cat's

a savage, a fighter.

We walk through windswept palms
and calls of exotic birds,
those birds who sleep all day

and sing all night, such
beautiful irony. And you
beautiful American, I want you

to buy me sunset daiquiris,
and white bikinis,
I want you to bruise me

softly with the blinds open.
Smuggle that cat home
howling the whole way.

Haunting the House

Uneasy trespass, yours is the face that guilts me to modesty.
No one's hands will ever hold mine without illicit significance,
without waking the dead. The one who gave me my poetry
and the one who took it away, the one who gave me back to myself
and all the simple men in between with good intentions.
They beat nightly under my floorboards.

In dreams my house is always falling apart,
plaster dropping away like flesh from the bone,
revealing the skeletal frame, intimacies
I'm embarrassed to see. But I've got a knack
for not seeing, for ignoring the elephant.
The market isn't quite right for selling, I say.
Let's play it cool and see what happens, I can wait.

There once was a girl who wanted to be a woman
and so she bargained with a man for the cure and made it so
and she swallowed her birth control daily and made it so
and she lived in a consequence of her own decisions
(or lack thereof) and it was so.
But now I'm broken in, but now I'm heavyhearted.
But now. I can wait.

About the Author

Erin Cisney is a graduate of Franklin & Marshall College and currently resides in Pennsylvania with her husband and two sons.

About the Press

Unsolicited Press is a small publisher in Portland, Oregon.

www.ingramcontent.com/pod-product-compliance
Lightning Source LLC
Chambersburg PA
CBHW030136100526
44591CB00009B/683